I0157852

# One Hundred Fifty Sonnets

## Kevin Davidson

*Now my eyes were fixed again*
*Upon my lady's face. And with my eyes,*
*my mind drew back from any other thought.*
　　　　　　　　　—Dante *Paradiso*


　*—To M.L.*

ISBN: 978-0-9969986-7-3

Cover image: *Beatrice and Virgil*, illustrated by Gustave Dore
from his series on Dante's Divine Comedy

Cover and book design by Mary Jo Loboda

Hillside Education
4/5 Bidwell Hill Road
Lake Ariel, PA 18436
www.hillsideeducation.com

# CONTENTS

# SONNET 1

I put my hand to pen and paper blank
With all the lover's art that I possess
To trace my love and God to thank,
And pray your love for me it grows not less.
I sing that you may let your heart relent,
And love again with fragrant morning new;
Rekindle now the flame that's almost spent
And make again a burning heart in you
    And yet my words are phantom-faint and weak;
    They fall too short and seem to me too base.
    They cannot show the color of your cheek,
    And cannot tell of all your kindest grace.
    Oh Muse come quickly, softy as a dove
    And lend me words that I might win her love.

# SONNET 2

I do confess the wrongs I've done to you.
Of such offense my guilt I gladly find
And years of penance would I gladly do,
If penance now could change your heart and mind.
For just as great Achilles in his wrath,
Enacted justice, friend and foe the same,
Refused all loves and favored justice path;
So you refuse to love with righteous claim.
    But as the Savior bled upon His tree,
    And His forgiveness whispered till the end;
    I pray you whisper words as sweet to me,
    And send me not away, but justice bend.
    For those who love by justice, cold and dried;
    They love as if our God had never died.

# SONNET 3

My love, my heart was hiding furtive shy
And slipped behind the shadows dim with fear.
My heart it walked not boldly 'neath the sky,
And to your light it came not ever near.
My eyes were lit with dying evening light,
And only saw the sun there slipping west
To leave the world to dim and dwind'ling night;
And dying light was mirrored in my chest.
  But you my love have brought the morning new
  With hues of gleaming grace both bright and bold.
  I am made new with just the sight of you
  With breaking dawn and rays of burning gold.
   I pray you not now veil your blushing grace,
  But let me see again your morning face.

# SONNET 4

Your mercy is a gently spreading spring,
And like the spring you melt the winter's claws,
And cause each cold and saddened heart to sing,
And every frozen heart it heals and thaws.
Your mercy is the silken lighted moon
That casts its gentle grace throughout the night;
And 'gainst the poisoned black remains immune,
And fills my heart again with softest light.
  I pray you leave me not in winter's cold,
  But bring you spring and mercy's soft'ning melt.
  I pray you leave me not in nightly hold,
  But let your mercy's light be in me felt.
   I pray you bring your mercy down on me
  And from my darkened guilt now set me free.

# SONNET 5

I saw my love go waking in the morn;
And yet I saw her clothed in evening light.
She walked alone as with a sadness torn,
As evening stars before the fall of night.
Her eyes were filled with sorrow yet unspilled,
And beauty with a sadness mingled there;
So bright was she and yet with shadows filled,
But by her brilliant tears she seemed more fair.
For as the trees in saffron flashing red
They show their beauty in their ardent death,
As always beauty is with sorrow wed;
So too her beauty sighed with sorrow's breath.
 The brilliance of her shadow pains me more
 To know that I'm the cause of shades she wore.

# SONNET 6

Perhaps I've wronged you, Love, so much you'd say
You would no longer love and would me gone.
And right you'd be to wish I would not stay,
I have not earned your love, this is forgone.
But speaking so of love it does seem low.
And makes all love seem as a counting pain.
For I to brother's aid do gladly go,
But go for love itself and not to gain.
No son can earn his mother's care and love;
And friend does not but love to win his friend;
And no man earns the Holy lighted Dove,
For love is given freely till the end.
 And by our sins we all do forfeit trust,
 Yet still we love though it may seem unjust.

# SONNET 7

Now it might seem I make an idol out of you
To set enshrined within my ardent heart,
And there devote my praise and all I do,
And set you high up in a world apart.
Perhaps you say I see a goddess bright,
Who's glimpsed sometimes 'round mountain spring and glen,
And burns with brilliance as with heavens light;
Who's gentle beauty's light surpasses men.
  But I make not an idol out of you;
  Your beauty gleams with you and God above.
  The light He lends is lit in mirrors blue,
  And in my love of you; my God I love.
  And so think not I set you up too high
  But know I see in you where grace does lie.

# SONNET 8

When Adam took the apple for his own
And lost the gift of lover's purest heart;
Then sin was writ on every human bone,
And sin it is that tears all loves apart.
Now only by the gifted grace of God
Can man again find love so washed and clean,
And every love, devoid of grace, is flawed,
All blackened, twisted, cruel and graceless mean.
  If as you say your love for me is pure
  Then it was gifted you from God above.
  And thus seems well to God that love endure,
  For by His hand we first were moved to love.
  So would you now deny this gift to you,
  And call this greatest gift of love untrue?

# SONNET 9

Within our hearts we made a garden fair;
Tween walls of iv'ry, set with golden lace.
We tended there our love with gentle care,
And watered all with gleaming nectared grace.
And there we walked among the blooming trees,
And there we waited long to eat the fruits,
And wandered where our willing feet did please
To tend our love and grow its deep'ning roots.
But now the winter's come with icy breath
And all our labor's gone to heartless frost.
Our garden's ringed about with frozen death
And all our fruit in early ripeness lost.
But by your mercy spring might come once more;
Our garden could be fairer than before.

# SONNET 10

Outside me hope is hounded, chased away
Where once was spring there's not but icy bleak,
And frosty shades of sorrow 'round me lay,
And chill me through and make me frozen weak.
Without your fragrant flame of warming light
My heart is left to winter's drifting snow,
And sharpened winds about me blow each night,
And 'neath the ice my heart it cannot grow.
And yet inside I keep my fires feed,
And keep my hope alive and burning still.
For hope will burn when all is frozen dead;
A flame no wind or winter's cold can kill.
And so with hope my heart does burn for you,
And stays still lit till spring does come anew.

# SONNET 11

I do not write these songs to please your mind;
I labor not to smoothly flatter you.
For words as those are loved and left behind
And will not make our waning love as new.
I do not write these songs for glory's sake;
I seek no notice for my humble songs.
For every pride on earth will fade or break
And cannot strengthen love or mend my wrongs.
  Instead I write that you might see again
  And now recall the love you had for me,
  And sigh for all the things that might have been
  And know again the things that might still be.
  I write my songs to break your heart of stone,
  And grow again the seeds of love we've sown.

# SONNET 12

The sun is far too brazen in its light,
And hammers heavy 'gainst the scorchèd ground,
And rages raw within his burning might,
And from him there's no shelter to be found.
The moon arrays herself in gaudy dress
With sickly sweet perfumes and jewelry vain,
Yet by her gaudy pride she shines the less
And in her silken light does wax and wane.
  Your light, my love, is soft and more demure;
  Your blushing brilliance far more kind and fair;
  And shines with subtle, simple fragrance pure,
  Both light and gentle shadow mingled there.
  And in your shades of softened azure hue
  I see a deeper brilliance bound in you.

# SONNET 13

This world is like a cold and lonesome road,
And every day becomes a weary, marching trudge.
All bowed and bent beneath this heavy load
I stumble blindly through the freezing sludge.
And every day I walk more slowly on
Without the hope of rest or coming end.
And every light I see seems pale and wan
And cannot see beyond the turning bend.
   Yet with the eyes of love we clear our sight;
   And see the purpose for the pains we feel;
   And with the help of love our burden's light;
   And every bruise this world inflicts will heal.
   Would you deny the loving help I'd give,
   And would on lonesome roads you rather live?

# SONNET 14

I know my words are useless as a knife
That's worn with rust and over use of age,
Though once was keen and shone with sharpened life
It now is dull as words upon this page.
Ulysses old, on one last voyage west,
He strove in vain for one more deed of fame;
So to my words with youthful strength were blessed
But now grow weak and broken, old and lame.
My words are winds against your weary back
That coldly blow while you endure till spring.
But though my words are weak and strength still lack
I'll not now cease but lift my voice and sing.
   Let not my words so pass unheeded by
   But hear me in my lonesome lover's cry.

# SONNET 15

And still I carry on my sighing way,
And holding yet within my heart a light
Of hope for love and your return one day,
And when I'll see the ending of this night.
I onward go my footsteps slow and tired,
Your mem'ry weighs me down and I am bent.
And still within my chest my heart is fired,
It yet beats strong and hale though badly rent.
And still there breathes in me a hope to find
The day when I will see my suff'ring's fruit
All ripened there within your heart and mind;
For still there lives in you my loving root.
    But frosts they come before the fruit is hung;
    My words are so dismissed before they're sung.

# SONNET 16

So like the setting of the sun are you
That leaves the world awash in rosy light;
A crimson blush beneath your eyes of blue;
Your eyes, like evening stars, hold back the night.
Though from the north the hardened wind does rage,
It stops still short confounded by your calming
Your warmth it fills my heart and mind and page,
And fills me all with hues both soft and clear.
    But night has come and you are gone away;
    The northern wind it screams across my sky,
    And I have only hope for coming day
    When you return and heed my heart-rent cry.
So rise again and light once more my heart
Before the night it tears me all apart.

# SONNET 17

The setting sun has washed the world in gold
And spreads the sky with gently burning light
When in my arms and heart it's you I hold;
For lover's eyes are ever clear and bright.
And as we sit, we two together here
The beauty of the world more brilliant seems:
Unstained by sin or any darkened fear,
And all is as within my dearest dreams.
   But I have lost the dappled damson sky,
   And every song is out of tune and pale.
   The road is long and dark and dreary dry,
   And now I see as through a teary veil.
   Return to me, my love, my heart and eyes
   That once again I'll see the dappled skies.

# SONNET 18

My ship is tossed and wearied by the sea.
The masts are broke, the sails asunder torn,
The crew all dead and washed away but me;
And I, a helpless captain am forlorn.
The wind and waves against me concord make,
And whisper words despairing in my ears.
They wrack my boat and battered bearing shake,
And now not I but sea me wayward steers.
   But you, my sails, my stalwart strength of ship,
   Have broke the masts that rigged us close and tight,
   And left me foundered here to turn and tip
   Defenseless 'gainst the brutal storming night.
   Oh God rebuild the masts that bear my boat,
   And give me sails that homeward I may float.

# SONNET 19

How fragrant is the morning, new each day.
Its seems as if there's not but hope ahead.
And all the world has slept the dark away,
And all things sing and rise from restful bed.
The sun and hope and love they dawn again
With gifted grace to raise the fallen heart
And right the capsized drowning souls of men,
To make a braver, stronger lover's start.
With each new day again my hope I find,
And once again I strive and strain for you.
The night reveals it's all in vain behind
But morning brings me songs of hope anew.
   Till my last day I'll hope for you again,
    And think not on the darkness that has been.

# SONNET 20

There's no one wants to hear my tale so told,
Nor yet have I as yet a tale to tell;
For mine is not of ventures brave or bold,
But only loving you and how I fell.
I am no captain clashing sword on sword;
Nor am I wise with stirring words to speak;
Nor have I here a noble ship to board;
But you're my claim to greatness bright and meek
   This only so to show my love and fire.
   Forgoing greatness for a simple life,
   For loving you is all I do desire;
   To live unknown without the taste of strife.
   Belittle not my gifts, but know them true,
   I've freely given all I am to you.

# SONNET 21

You are not great of stature, build or strength,
And in the world your acts not counted great.
Nor have you wisdom gained by years of length;
You are not rich in gold or fine estate.
My love your hand is gentle, soft and fair,
And some might even say your hand is weak.
And for the strife of men you have no care,
But only meekly turn your blushing cheek.
   Yet by your gentle hand I'm wrecked and slain;
   My heart is torn and cries in anguish deep.
   For by your love you cause the greatest pain,
   And make my rending heart to pine and weep.
   Remember in your hands you hold my heart,
   And smallest look can tear me all apart

# SONNET 22

Beneath the sun my heart was singing glad,
And sang of love and saffron feathered grace.
I sang with you through all the days we had,
And gazed with ceaseless joy upon your face.
Below the clouds my heart was wailing keen
And wept for loss of love and loss of you.
I've washed my face in tears till all is clean
And every day my cry of anguish grew.
   But now my heart is silent, still and calm,
   It moves not quick to joy or crashing tears.
   For hope is as a gently soothing balm
   That cleanses pride and cools the burning fears.
   My heart is now content to wait and stay
   With quiet hope that you will turn my way.

# Sonnet 23

Your hands are small and clean of evil stain,
And gentle in their soft caressing touch.
Such hands as yours cannot cause ill or pain,
And all you touch is gentle made as such.
Your lips soft and sweet like soothing wine,
And speak no evil words but softly pray.
And softly stay all doubt when they touch mine,
And all you kiss comes sweet as springing May.
So great your love when you release it so
That none can bar its way or make it turn,
And yet is humbler far than man can know,
And makes all hearts about you brightly burn.
   So let you love come softly on me now
   With all the gentle grace that you endow.

# Sonnet 24

I won't deny I've sinned and sorely fell,
I'll own my wrongs and stand the blame you place.
I ner' was one to hide my good and sins as well,
But I'm no worse than any man you'll face.
Now you expected much of all the love I gave,
And expectations are not wrong at all,
But man is fallen, tempted till the grave;
For all our expectations we will fall.
   Though expectation fails as did before,
   There is still hope that man will rise again;
   Shrug off his heavy sins to walk once more,
   Despite the darkened places we have been.
   Expect not pure perfection in all things,
   But hold your hope, for hope is what love brings.

# Sonnet 25

I have on wings of softest silken love
Ascended through the breathless fog of earth.
And with you gazed on lights of bliss above,
And countless moments spent of countess worth.
We two, we sang above the world below.
We sat and sang our love beneath the sky,
And softly bent our hearts and minds to know,
And sing each other's songs until we die.
   But oh how far I've fallen from those heights,
   And all for want of faith and constancy:
   Your wings were burnt by sharp unclouded lights;
   While mine were heavied by the raging sea.
   But ah the middle course we nearly missed,
   And lost the wings that sprang when first we kissed.

# Sonnet 26

Around the loss of you my mind is wound;
I sit all night and think on what has been.
Unmoved by friendly touch or gentle sound
I think of you, and think of you again.
They say such leaden moods are wrong to keep.
They say it's wrong to so prolong the pain
And let this darkness 'round me grow more deep,
Or let my heart begin to dim and wane.
   But wrong it seems to quickly leave behind
   The pain of loss for just appearance sake,
   Or forfeit love for ease of heart and mind;
   For then an untrue lover I would make.
   I'll not distract myself from losing you,
   But gladly let my heart be torn in two.

# SONNET 27

The roots of love are planted well and deep
When first the lover digs to plant the seed,
And deep within the heart is lain to sleep,
And there to wait for God's sweet light to heed.
To plow the heart is labor full of pain;
The blade that breaks and turns the hardened earth
Will dig and cut the heart till open lain,
And only then may seed there come to worth.
But if this seed is thrown to untilled ground
Where plowman has not passed his cutting shear
Such love will die before its roots it's found;
And burned by lust or chilled with freezing fear.
So plow your heart in readiness to sow,
For love it comes at times we never know.

# SONNET 28

My wrongs are heavy, hung about my neck
And drag me down to dim and dusty earth,
And all the good I've done may fall to wreck
And all my acts bereft of purest worth.
But I am just a humble, earthly man
And have my virtues, great and small in weight
For man has fallen since the world began,
No matter how the man be small or great.
But would you love a man by sin unstained,
Who wears his grinning mask with lies for pride?
For all such hearts have truth and beauty feigned,
And in their hearts a deeper sin do hide.
But I'll not hide my faults 'neath whitened masks
But humbly strive despite as heaven asks.

# SONNET 29

Each day I see you walking, passing by,
And every day more beautiful by far
That at your beauty I would surely cry;
As bright as sunset with an azure star.
Each day I'm made more weak of heart's resolve,
The battle grows more frantic in my mind:
To fly to you or let your love dissolve;
By day no resting from this war I find.
  So when the weary night has come to stay;
  Then to my sleep I fly to run from you,
  But there in all my dreams you softly say:
  "I love you still, my love, my long life through."
  And so 'tween days and dream there's no escape
  From loving you in flesh or phantom shape.

# SONNET 30

They say the unrequited lover's love
Is not, in truth, a wholesome love at all,
And is no graceful gift from God above,
And so is bound by fate to fail and fall.
They call such lovers useless, cold and dull,
For from the world of truth they hide with fears,
And all their minds with myths of love are full;
While all their poems fall on deafest ears.
  But rather would I sing so unreturned
  Than sing untuned and leaking logic lead.
  And call you Christ a poet-fool who burned
  With love so unrequited without heed?
  I'd be a fool and love without demand
  Than force my love to take me by the hand.

# SONNET 31

I'm now resigned to unrequited love,
And find myself content without your hand,
And love this beauty more that I sing of
Despite the spaces that between us stand.
And though such love indeed seems long and bleak
I'll not allow resilient heart be sold.
Though it be maimed and broken, faint and weak
I'll keep my love still burning bright and bold.
　For I have found my peace in patient prayer,
　Content to let my God now do his will.
　My desperate plight does make my plea more fair
　And all the ears of God my prayer does fill.
　I pray my unrequited love in you
　With hope that God will let our love renew.

# SONNET 32

They say that poets' words are fine and sweet
So well he speaks that all do stand in awe
And wonder at the fragrant metered feet,
That all might see the beauty that he saw.
And yet they say he speaks untrue, too high,
And all he says is just ideal, no more.
His words are wishes all, or else he lie,
And tempts the heart with dark and evil lore.
　They only say so for they don't believe
　And don't know love and beauty as they ought.
　But poets find the secret heart and weave
　That binds our hearts. He knows the things we've sought.
　So cast my loving songs away with care
　For they are true despite, their beauty fair.

# SONNET 33

I would my love were pure and snowy white;
For such a love is love as you deserve.
The love I have to is not so clear and bright,
But muddied through with sin and self-reserve.
And all I do for you is mixed with me.
I only see you through my human eyes,
And only see in parts what whole should be.
I love you more then less, and fall then rise.
My love for you is only human love
And bound to fail and fall, perhaps undone.
For though my love is gifted from above
It's dirtied by my use and time's long run.
   I would my love were Christ's, with fair demure,
   For then my love would grow, and grow more pure.

# SONNET 34

My eyes have found and held your color clear
And know your shape and caref'lly trace your face.
Your voice is sought like treasure to my ear
That slips your lips and with your soul is lace.
And when my fingertips they touch you soft
My fingers all rejoice to know you so.
Your fragrance lifts my heart so light aloft
As warm and soft as when the south winds blow.
The taste of you is like a golden wine
That soothes my dried and slowly dying heart.
I know you all by these both fair and fine,
Though by these do I only know in part.
   But by my love I know you – heart and soul.
   For only love can know beloved whole.

# SONNET 35

I lay last night all wrapped in deep browed sleep,
And to me came from gentle angels' race,
Or devil's tempting hiss and fing'ring creep;
A dream of you in all your gleaming grace.
I dreamt I saw you standing softly there
Your face was lit with lover's smiling light
And light was laced into your falling hair,
You said your heart for me it still burned bright.
   Was this the will of God: to give me hope,
   And light my sinking heart back home to you?
   Or was it just temptation that I grope,
   To build false hope in me as devils do?
   If from my God or devil I don't know,
   I do not know, I do not know! But Oh!

# SONNET 36

I've now engaged my praise of you not long
And still my searching words are all in vain.
For still I feel the weakness of my song,
But such is but a lover's pining pain.
For like the waves that strike the rocky shore
My words are useless 'gainst your beauty bright.
Against you words are but a savage roar:
The sea will break for all her rage and might.
If I were wise I'd turn, surrender now
I'd still my pen in failure's silent rest,
And not on you the shame of art allow,
And not dishonor so what God has blessed.
   But I'm a fool and will speak useless on
   Till all my loving words are spent and gone.

# SONNET 37

Oh Love, that we were here together wed,
And I could breathe my words to you in flesh.
Instead I write these things my heart has said
To make your waning love for me afresh.
Oh Love, if I could see your smiling face;
If I could touch the softness for your hand;
And breathe again the warmth and light; your grace;
That 'tween us did not sit this grim command.
   For then my heart that's beaten, broken bound
   Could so shrug off the blinding, choking dark,
   Rekindled would I be, and raised from ground;
   And coals of soul in me could then find spark.
I'll find no peace until I find you Love,
Or hope no joy until I've gone above.

# SONNET 38

Each day I spend in wondering where you are,
And thinking on the good that we once were,
And call back joys and tears from mem'ries far;
From contemplation can my mind not stir.
By dark my heart is haunted by your love
Unbidden to my dreams you come by night
Then wing away as softly as a dove,
And leave me lonesome by the morning light.
   By day I find no rest from mem'ry's pain,
   By night I find no rest in haunting dreams.
   These mem'ries in me writhe and outward strain
   So sorrow wrung my heart it's rending seams.
      And so on earth I cannot rest my mind
      Unless again your soothing love I find.

# SONNET 39

My heart and mind and body ache and groan,
And beaten by the woes of world and time,
And to the ground by sin again I'm thrown;
My heart too broken now again to climb.
My wounds are cut too deep and will not heal
I cannot by my power make me new
And cannot sooth the burning pain I feel
And all is vain whatever else I do.
But by your love I'll learn again to rise,
Shake off this weight of sordid love and stand.
I'll be made whole by gazing on your eyes
And lifted by your gently raising hand.
For only by your love may I be whole,
And only you can sooth my wearied soul.


# SONNET 40

I here again renew my lover's suit;
I ask again for your forgiveness soft.
I know that I am at your sorrow's root.
I ask again your mercy from aloft
That you may love again as you once did;
I beg again on bended lover's knee,
I ask let not your love from me be hid.
Instead I pray you hear again my plea.
Though you remain unmoved at hearing this
And set yourself above my humble prayer
Remember now the sweetness of that bliss
That we both shared when love was young and fair.
I only ask that you consider still
And let my songs your heart now fill.

# SONNET 41

I see that by the coolness of your eye
You've steeled yourself to love me now no more
And let our love go quiet, slipping by,
And all  the love you have you will ignore.
With firm resolve you look away from me
And set your gaze upon some far off place
As if I were a sight that you'd not see,
And would not see the love within my face.
My pleas are vain and all unheard by you,
Your ears are deaf to reason, deaf to love;
You would not change whatever I may do.
My only hope is heaven's help above.
    I pray my God to change your heart and mind
    That you not leave your truest love behind.

# SONNET 42

I too have tried to leave my love behind;
To no more feel the lover's joy or pain.
I've tried to put you from my heart and mind,
For all I do it seems to be in vain.
I told myself I loved you not at all
And from your mem'ry I did try to run.
And though I could not run I still could crawl,
And so I hoped to once again be done.
    And yet I found I was more tightly bound
    By cords of love than I have ever known;
    For in my love of you my self is found
    So close, through binding love, have we two grown.
    To cut out you would cut myself from me,
    And man cannot so self-despising be.

# SONNET 43

Some part of you, I know, exists through me.
Some part of you is bound up in my soul.
Some part of who you are will never be
Unless again with me are you made whole.
The self that you've become is torn apart,
It's thrown away and with me cast aside.
You've ripped apart the fabric of your heart
And now you ask that something new abide.
    But if, indeed, you want to be made new,
    (Become a different self than you have been)
    Then cut me from your heart and soul and you
    And with a newer self you'll love again.
    I pray you not so cast aside your self,
    Or leave it hidden on some dusty shelf.

# SONNET 44

You say that all I do is all for me
And this I don't deny as all untrue;
For from our love of self we're never free.
I am in everything I do for you.
In every gift there's double benefit;
The gift is meant to please receiver whole
And gives the giver joy in giving it
For by my gift I help to grace my soul.
    And so this song is not for me alone
    For both our sakes I write this verse for you.
    It pleases me when I my heart have shown
    And gifts you with the things I write and do.
    And you as well would help yourself and me
    If once again we could together be.

# Sonnet 45

Let not my mem'ry quickly slip from mind,
Or washed away in time's cold river's wave.
With time and distance put me not behind,
And don't forget the joy that once I gave.
Is now my face a half remembered dream,
That's seen at night and left in shadows there;
Forgotten with the light of new day's gleam,
Forgotten now where once you used to care?
I ask that you remember me anew
And hold as cherished treasure in your mind
The thought that I am waiting here for you.
Remember  how the guiding stars aligned.
Remember once you loved me well and full,
Let not such mem'ries grow too old and dull.

# Sonnet 46

I could remember of my time with you
Those things that cast you in a poorer light,
I could remember many things it's true,
And yet I only see what's good and bright.
I could recall the times you did me wrong,
And all the ways we went so far astray.
I could recall the nights so bleak and long,
And yet I only see a brighter day.
I could think back and only see the dark,
And count the mounting missteps that I've made,
And count the odds that make my love seem stark,
And yet before my love this all does fade.
I ask you now, my love, to do the same;
Remember gently when you speak my name

# SONNET 47

I know I've wronged you, this I do concede,
I have not won your love nor earned regard,
I know because of me your heart does bleed,
Your mem'ry of me have I only marred.
I know that now you see me as a scar;
Now healed and closed it soon begins to fade
And all the mem'ries now do seem so far:
So you forget the mem'ries that we've made.
  I pray you not to shut your mem'ry's door
  On all our love and joy and kindness yet,
  Remember how I looked at you before.
  Remember me with love and not regret.
  Remember me, that's all that you can do;
  Remember me, that all I ask of you.


# SONNET 48

Remember me when you are old and gray;
When bitter age has stolen joy from life;
When all your loves have past and gone away,
When you are left alone, or widowed wife.
Remember me when all the days are long;
When every night's a cold and lonesome road;
When no one here can sing your loving song,
And wilted all the seed of love you sowed.
Remember me when you are left alone;
When other easy love's have gone and past;
When false has every other lover grown,
And all their masks removed, revealed at last.
  Remember I still love you on and on,
  And I will love you still when all is gone.

# Sonnet 49

The time may change and we grow old and die,
And though the very mouth of hell be wide,
And all the rivers of the world run dry,
My love will stand there steady by your side.
The light may fade and leave us all in dark;
But though the stars come crashing down to earth
My love will kindle still a lasting spark
To shine in us with fixèd holy worth.
And though the sun above may melt the stones,
And leave this world a godforsaken waste
And though there be but barest  flesh on bones
The cool and soothing drink of love we'll taste.
For I will love you till we are no more;
Until the final closing of the door.

# Sonnet 50

Now as you say I've done great wrong by you,
And by my sins it seems I love you less;
For if perfection tests a love as true,
Then 'gainst a perfect love I do transgress.
And if you say I've failed in love somehow,
And shown a lack of tender touch and care;
Then to this claim I do admit and bow,
And for my wrongs my penance I will bear.
  But do not say that I have loved you not
  For I have loved you true despite my fault,
  Despite the heavy sorrow that I've brought,
  And love you even when I seem to halt.
  For sin and failure turn me not away
  And still I love you more than I can say.

# Sonnet 51

Yes, time and time again I've failed your love,
As time and time again I fall to sin.
And time again I'm saved by God above,
As time again your love I have to win.
But time and time again you've wronged me too,
And time and time again I must forgive.
Forgiving's only what all lovers do
If they're to love and with each other live.
   Forgive me then for though I've wronged you so
   That we may learn what love demure demands.
   For by such sacrifice our love will grow,
   And with forgiving love we'll join our hands.
   Let us proceed in mending love with grace
   That we may see again as face to face.

# Sonnet 52

The wrongs I've done to you are great I know,
And I am not alone in suff'ring loss,
For you have lost me, even as you go,
This parting pain is to us both a cross.
The hardship that I've laid on you is great,
And every thought of me is filled with pain,
And bears you down with losing's heavy weight,
And every day's a heavyhearted strain.
   If we endure and both our wills do bend
   What greater love and grace could we now find?
   If we but see our suff'ring through the end,
   And love again and grow from pain behind.
   So take this suff'ring up with me and walk,
   And build our love again on solid Rock.

# SONNET 53

My love, your beauty is to me as light;
Just like the dawn when breaking o'er the hills,
That boldly grows to fill my darkened sight,
And makes me new when from the heavens spills.
Your light is gentle like the quiet moon
That's drifted through the world of light bereft;
As through my darkened heart is sweetly strewn,
And gives me hope when all my hope has left.
The stars are cast across the sky above,
So many there my eyes could go astray,
But through the lesser lights there shines your love;
A guiding mark that helps my course to stay.
   Do not then veil your light but brightly shine,
   And light this darkened world that's yours and mine.

# SONNET 54

My love, your beauty is to me as snow
With gentle touch you fall from heaven's height,
And softly come to wrap my ground below,
And make this earth reflect the sun more bright.
Or as the sweetly falling rain in spring
You softly kiss me, make me all anew
With all the warmth and breath you softly bring;
Again each year am I remade with you.
   From tempests both renewing beauties fall;
   Such beauty only comes from storms and strife.
   So through you tempest I do cry and call;
   Let fall your rain, your snow, renew my life.
   Do not within your tempest wait and stay;
   Let beauty fall and round me softly lay.

# Sonnet 55

My love, your beauty is to me like sails
That bear my little boat of life to shore.
Though bent by violent storms and raging gales
You forward draw my hopes, and dreams, and more.
Though torn and patched through dreadful conflicts long,
And faded by the beating, burning sun,
Despite the ways I've lead on headings wrong
You bear me still till all is past and done.
I ask you still to bear me even now
Though I have gone astray, and turned off course.
And leave me not a sinking, unrigged prow,
But hear my prayer and heed my true remorse.
So leave me not alone upon this sea
Where I am lost without a sail to me.


# Sonnet 56

My love, you have become my cornerstone;
My stone foundation for my love and life,
And I would build on you and grace alone,
And shelter there within our love from strife.
And on you love could stand immobile, strong,
Though beaten hard by tempests time will throw.
The love I build on you could last as long
As we two in our love together grow.
But since you've gone my house is tossed and shakes.
It sinks in sand and leans from side to side,
It barely stands the wind that on it breaks,
It creaks and moans and all begins to slide.
Without your love this house is just a wreck,
But were you here this ruin we could check.

# SONNET 57

Your sun has set upon my hills, my heart,
With one last brilliant flash of ardent fire,
And in that moment tears my world apart,
And rips me 'tween my mind and heart's desire.
In parting painting all the sky in flame
Unseen in noonday's over eager strains.
For now you burn and never will the same;
Such light as burns is fueled with love and pains.
So you are burning in your leaving now
With brilliant beauty as the dying light,
That burns upon the sky's deep dark'ning brow;
So you are burning, going down to night.
 I have no words to tell how bright you seem,
 And all the gentled hues that from you stream.

# SONNET 58

I once was free and owned my heart and mind.
I made my way and found my joy alone.
No care I had for home and hearth behind,
And home and hearth ahead were not my own.
I wandered round this world so free of care
The world was all my own and gave me joy
To me my life seemed bright and rightly fair
And bore no thought for love 'tween girl and boy.
 But when I saw the light of love in you
 My heart and feet stopped still in rest at last.
 I lost my heart and will and all I do,
 I took the chains you gave me, bound me fast.
 These chains of love are sweet and fit me well,
 And chains as these will save my soul from hell.

# SONNET 59

I am now bound to you and to your heart
As if between us were a tighten string.
Though we still stand some distance here apart,
This string between us still a song does sing.
And at each note I hear your heart and mind
As played upon some golden gilded harp.
I feel each time you pluck your meaning kind
And feel your pain in me both dull and sharp.
For all you think and do it strikes a cord,
And when you're out of tune I am as well.
And you can hear my soul when all discord,
As you have heard at every time I fell.
  So let us tune together now our string,
  And play a song as those in heaven sing.


# SONNET 60

When I remember that we two are part'd,
And all the love we shared is cast away;
And when I think on all the joy we've start'd,
And how for this there's much I have to pay
I feel my heart is ripped apart and burned
As if some loveless hand had torn it out.
The world I see is then to darkness turned,
And all I know as true is turned to doubt.
  Yet parting was a blessing in disguise,
  For now I see you as I never did.
  And parting has but cleared my blinded eyes,
  And nothing now is from my vision hid.
For now I know I love you more than life
Which makes the parting keener than a knife.

# Sonnet 61

When first our love was set aside to wait,
And put away upon a dusty shelf
Until a time ordained by you and fate;
When I am cleansed and you again yourself;
I did not know what I should do or say
To win you back or gain again your love.
I did not know a way to wrongs repay.
My prayers remained unanswered from above.
I cast about, but means were scarce to find;
In vain my hopes in you I did confide.
I searched through every means of heart and mind,
But fell upon the ground and nearly died.
    The answer came then clear to me and true:
    I'll die to me and live again in you.

# Sonnet 62

Our love was not a little candle flame
Whose light is lost with just the smallest breath,
And all is left in dark without a name:
Our love will not go quiet to its death.
Oh no. Our love was as a fervent blaze
That warmed us two and those who walked nearby,
And would have lasted out through all our days,
And though the wind blew fierce it would not die.
    But now you want to put this fire out,
    And use whatever means you have to you –
    Though this desire I do surely doubt –
    But carry on in what you think you do.
Though you may crash with waves as does the sea
You cannot douse the flames you've lit in me.

# Sonnet 63

I feel again my keen despair is come
To darken all I think of me and you,
And turn all other joys all cold and numb,
To stifle all I thought was bright and true.
And like some dimming fog from hell's cold land
It creeps upon me low and stealthy slow,
And reaching out a cold and clutching hand;
It reaches sure for all I love and know.
And in its depth I am become as blind
To truth and pain and darkened reason's light.
Again I'm trapped in things I've left behind,
And will not hope to see my heart made right.
  But still there springs eternal in my chest;
  The hope that love might in your heart still rest.

# Sonnet 64

I know it seems I think I need you here;
That I depend on you for breath I take,
And cannot now exist without you near,
But this of course would be a grave mistake.
For neither you nor I need love so much
That we would cease to be if so deprived.
For I will still be man without your touch,
And such dependencies are all contrived.
  But if we two were one, together bound
  Then how much more we'd be than when alone.
  Our love would then be ever greater found,
  And never would it fail or be outgrown.
  For two as one transcends this mortal love,
  And reaches up with Christ and God above.

# Sonnet 65

I know that hearing this is harsh and hard,
My words are not all sweet and bright to take,
And leave your fragile heart and mind well scarred,
And sorrow in you do they only make.
Your words as well have quickly cut me deep
For they reveal the faults I never knew
And fills my waking thoughts and dreams in sleep
Because I know them all as right and true.
　　But by this searing pain within our minds
　　We two will grow to love each other more.
　　For by this pain the humble lover finds
　　A truer, deeper love than was before.
　　So let us help and guide the other's soul
　　That we may learn to love each other whole.


# Sonnet 66

When man and woman are together wed,
And bound to one another two as one;
In flesh the two are one until they're dead,
And share each other's selves in all that's done.
As trees that twine there branches overhead,
Though from their separate roots have sprung and grown,
So wound that which is which cannot be said,
And live there locked till all their days have flown.
　　But I say more: instead as rivers flow,
　　And mingle all that's theirs and give complete,
　　And as a whole new river they do go,
　　With all their waters mixed to one replete.
　　So lovers' make one body, heart, and soul,
　　And neither have themselves as one and whole.

# SONNET 67

I ask you not to love because I'm kind
And comfort those that in me solace sought
If so then leave this half formed love behind
For love for kindness sake is all for not.
And do not love because I sooth your pain
Or give you all your heart and mind do need
Such love does all too quickly wax and wane.
And withers with the first misstep, misdeed.
　For I, a fallen man, will always fall,
　And when my kindness slips your love will too
　Instead I ask you: love me for my all
　Not simply for the things I do for you.
　For partial love as this will pass away
　But loving whole will here forever stay.

# SONNET 68

I ask you not to love for pity's sake;
Because alone I'm left with broken heart,
And from my sinking sorrow cannot break,
Or cannot forward make a heartfelt start.
And love me not from up above on high,
And reaching down to give me bread to eat,
Or wipe the tears that desperation cry,
Or lift me up upon my shaking feet.
　Your loving help I need I know it's true;
　And I am bettered by your love and aid.
　But you are bettered when I give to you,
　We both by love are better lovers made.
　So let us love as equals with respect,
　For pity loves not goodness, just defect.

# Sonnet 69

I ask you not to love because I do,
Or some imagined duty feel to me.
Such love is only loss to me and you,
Instead your love should all be given free.
And feel not guilty if you love me not;
You've done no wrong by lacking passion's light.
For love's not forced or by some duty wrought
Such love is not imbued with graces bright.
   But if you love me too with heart complete
   Then call to me with longing in your voice,
   And run to me with passion quickened feet,
   And love me with the wholeness of your choice.
   So love me then with love and longing's flame,
   And not with duty by another name.

# Sonnet 70

The things I've done for you are gladly done,
And all were but to show my love for you.
Though small I meant my love in every one,
And I would show my love in all I do.
The greatest deed or just the smallest task
With care and kind devotion I will meet.
And I would gladly give what e'er you ask,
And all would seem to me as bright and sweet.
   But do not force my hand to give my gift
   For acts of love are mine to give and choose.
   Demanding love will only cause a rift,
   For I will see that you my love abuse.
     Yet I would give you all you want and need,
     And every dearest vein in me would bleed.

# SONNET 71

Till now you've lived your life upon a given line
Of straightened, finite breath and length
To here construct tween circles clear and fine;
A life that's proved as good with logic's strength.
Your path was ever paved both smooth and straight,
And clearly marked to you and on ahead,
And all you've had to do is simply wait,
For by a firm command you're forward lead.
   But were you now to love with passion full,
   And love me with a love of fire's heat
   You'd then shake off all loves of colors dull,
   And find you're made as new and now complete.
   On other colder love's you'd go to waste,
   But find in me a warm and wholesome taste.

# SONNET 72

The ghosts of who we were can still be seen;
In love they pass, not caring for our strife.
There walking still the streets where we have been,
These streets are filled with ghosts of fairer life.
I walk among them every day and night,
And hear their whispered words around me crowd.
These whispers sweep about me, airy, light,
And fill my ears with crying calling loud.
   But you and I are now become as ghosts,
   And pass each other by on deadened feet.
   Among the whisping crowding phantom hosts
   We walk without ourselves on earth complete.
     Our separated souls cannot find rest
     Until again with greater love we're blessed.

# SONNET 73

Before our parting on our separate ways
I loved you truly, more than anyone,
And still will truly love through all my days,
Until my life and all the world are done.
Perhaps my thoughts on love were then unclear
And though we two were tangled as a knot,
And mingled then with cold and doubting fear,
And path to purest love I blindly sought.
   But by our parting have I finally found
   The clear and lighted road of love and grace.
   And now by stronger bonds of love I'm bound,
   And truly see the beauty in your face.
   For from the pain of losing you I see,
   And have untangled all the knots in me.

# SONNET 74

Around my mind the frenzied winds do blow,
And rage against my fragile walls and door.
And with the night they only greater grow;
They lash at me with crazèd thrashing roar.
My house, my heart, is rent and battered, bent,
And torn apart by clawing tooth and nail.
The winds the world against my heart has sent
Around my heart and mind do plunge and wail.
   But you, my love, have strengthened these four walls,
   Have filled the chinks that wind can whistling find;
   Supported up my roof before it falls;
   Remade my house, my battered heart and mind.
   For in your love I do my shelter seek,
   And make myself again though I be weak.

## SONNET 75

The night is dark about my wearied heart,
Descended down from setting sun it fell,
And crept around me, kindly at the start,
Until it had me caught in black of hell.
The darkness reaches steady out to me
To snuff the lighted candle I have still,
Till only folds of deeper dark I see,
And crushes out the last small light of will.
  But you rekindle light of will I lack,
  And by your breath of love my flames will grow.
  And by its brilliance beats the darkness back,
  Till only light and you my heart does know.
  And soon this flame will grow into a blaze
  To fill my heart with light through all my days.

## SONNET 76

They say that I'm a lighted lamp that gleams,
And shines with warming hues of singing light,
That wraps all things with soft and lancing beams,
Revealing all the beauty fair and bright.
They say I shine into their darkness dim,
And warm the cold and darkened dying earth,
And fill their empty cup up to the brim
With light of love, renewing agèd worth.
  But all this light I show is lit by you;
  From light and life you've given me in love.
  For in me was your flame there kindled true;
  A gift of grace to you from God above.
  And this twice gifted light will in me burn
  For all the world to see and for it yearn.

# SONNET 77

My castle's walls are broad and stalwart high,
But by your beauty under siege and trapped.
And in these walls I've made I'll surely die
For by your beauty all my strength is sapped.
Against my walls your beauty takes assault,
And uses all its skill and deadly art.
And not for sake of pity will it halt,
For it has sworn to tear my walls apart.
  Have gentle mercy on my heart I plead
  For if you end this siege I'll swear my oath
  And so no more will by your beauty bleed;
  So saving love and blood,by mercy, both.
  I do surrender to your  fair attack,
  And from this love I'll not now hold me back.

# SONNET 78

With gaudy rings they do their hands adorn,
And hang their pounds of gold about the neck,
And cannot count the garish jewels they've worn;
So other beauties do their beauty wreck.
With complex trinkets of the highest cost
They hide themselves in gold and amethyst,
And in a sea of chains their beauty's lost,
And cover all themselves from heart to wrist.
  But you possess a beauty much more pure;
  Unstained by false additions to your light,
  And hold yourself with ease and fair demure;
  With modest shades you shine in hues more bright.
  For other beauties wear their gaudy fear,
  But I do hold you modest light more dear.

# SONNET 79

Oh Love there's nothing more that I can do
To spark in you a warm and loving light.
For all my kindest gifts are called untrue;
As if my acts was hidden from your sight.
Oh Love there's nothing more that I can say;
For all my words remain unheard and vain.
My every reasoned tact is thrown away,
And every plea for mercy ends in pain.
　There's nothing now that I can do but wait;
　There's nothing I can say to turn you back
　But pray my prayers for love come not too late,
　And be content despite my love and lack.
　And so I'm here content with just my prayer,
　Despite the way my heart does break and tear.


# SONNET 80

The cold and clawing winds are wrapped and whipped
And bring the snow with whitened fury low,
And from the earth the growing warmth is ripped
Till all is still and frozen, locked in snow.
And so my heart is frozen, dead and still,
And bit by winds from northern mountain peak.
By wint'ry rage I'm struck all through with chill,
And all in vain a warmth and light I seek.
　But you are as the rain of springing life
　Or as the spring itself within my heart;
　That melts away the snow and wint'ry strife,
　And gives the world again a second start.
　So let your spring come back from where you've been,
　And melt my heart and make me warm again.

# Sonnet 81

If love was as a river running strong
Then ours was broad, with currents coursing deep.
That sprung in rocky ground with trick'ling song,
And grew in valleys where the trees do sleep.
But you would dam our love and halt its strength,
And build a wall to hold the waters back.
And so cut short our river in its length,
And no more flow along this loving track.
   But dams are weak no matter what their size;
   Behind them rivers only pool and grow,
   And so the waters there in strength will rise,
   Till dam is broke or river overflow.
   No more can you so stop a river's course
   Than can you dam our love with all its force.

# Sonnet 82

Each year when winter comes with snow and ice
The trees all lose their color of their leaves.
For this is how their beauty pays the price;
As love is lost so all the world believes.
To all the world the trees are lost and dead
And dried as bones gone deathly gray and dark.
Their lives are done when all their leaves are shed:
So too our love has lost its living spark
   But with the spring the trees put forth their green,
   When hardened winter leaves the world at length.
   They were not dead but only so were seen,
   And by their death they're greater in their strength.
   So let our love grow stronger by its death,
   And grow again with greater life and breath.

# SONNET 83

When fire strikes with grim and deadly flame,
With roaring fury as some dragon's rage
It burns with heated vengeance none can tame,
Consuming all, the young and old of age.
 And when it's past and all the flames have left
Then all has perished 'neath the burning lash,
And all is burnt and black and life bereft.
So too our love is burnt and charred to ash.
   But when again the forest trees regrow
   They grow more lush and vibrant than before,
   And deeper hues of green and gold they show,
   And by this grim destruction grow much more.
   These ashes of our love will grow anew,
   And make our love much stronger than we knew.

# SONNET 84

The days have all become a barren waste;
A land devoid of water, scorched and dead,
And now for forty days I've not had taste
Of water cool, or broken fast with bread.
I walk alone upon this exile sand,
Not lost but aimless, wand'ring in this place.
I wait for you my love, my promise land,
And still before my eyes I see your face.
   But though I walk this desert's vastness through
   I walk my wand'ring way that I decrease
   And by this pain increase my love for you
   Though forty year may pass before release.
   And so I wait for you in deserts vast
   Until these fated forty days have past.

# SONNET 85

A tree that's grafted with another tree
Will grow a fruit that tastes of both the two,
And by their union will they better be:
As lovers wed, themselves will make anew.
Before the trees are grafted, two in one;
Before they grow as one and mix their fruits,
And share their lives so joined through storm and sun,
They both are cut down to their very roots.
   For only so by death are lovers wed.
   They let themselves be slain for sake of love,
   So all their staining fear and pride be shed;
   In death their love is joined with Christ's above.
   This parting now will surely kill us both,
   But let us pledge a true and purer oath.

# SONNET 86

Within a furnace heat, with fire's pain
And under hammer's heavy testing stroke
Is steel made strong – but still as steel remain –
By fire, death, and pain is strength awoke.
The sickened body undergoes the same
In facing death it now will longer last
And as the steel within the heated flame
Is made more strong and pure when sickness past.
So too all things must die to be reborn,
And all is brighter after bearing loss.
As night will end and then give way to morn,
As glory gained by hanging on the Cross.
   So too our love will by this death be strong,
   And we will sing a fairer brighter song.

# SONNET 87

My head is hot with burning fevered heat;
I shake and shiver, chilled through every bone,
And all my body pounds with quickened beat.
I'm sick and breathe my last with every moan.
My mind is twisted back and forth in me,
And moves with thoughts and notions not so deft,
And knows no longer what the truth may be.
I've gone insane, I have no reason left.
   I'm sick with love, for this I've gone insane.
   My mind and body are no longer sound,
   My love's infected every bleeding vein.
   For this disease no cure can e'er be found.
      My heart alone it still beats steady, true;
      My heart it beats in me and beats for you.

# SONNET 88

I see your face and figure kindly framed,
And pictures show your beauty almost true
With tender blush, as morning all inflamed
Against your eyes of deep and nightly blue.
Despite your captured features held and still
Such pictures wrong the beauty of you face,
And can't repeat the light your features spill,
And pictures can't your motion fully trace.
   But all the pictures show you half as well
   As mem'ries locked within my heart and mind.
   Such mem'ries hearts can never wholly quell
   And can't your fragrant beauty leave behind.
      I care not much for picture's rigid line,
      For you yourself are fair and far more fine.

# SONNET 89

I know you think my words are gilded truth,
As whispered nothings in your gentle ear,
And think I sweetly lie through every tooth,
And only say these things to keep you near.
You say my words are gleaming hammered gold
That touch you heart with fingers soft and slight,
But not a gleam of lighted truth do hold,
Nor weigh as much as truth but far too light.
  But this belief does mock my careful art,
  And so dismiss my every word and thought.
  And call as false the bleeding of my heart,
  For by these words my very love is wrought.
    And by this doubt you call yourself untrue,
    For all these words do claim the truth in you.

# SONNET 90

Your hair is trick'ling flame in ardent rush,
And wafts a warmth and fragrance round your head.
Your cheeks are brushed with warm and tender blush,
And lit as dawn and dusk, so softly red.
Your eyes are azure stars in midnight skies,
A bathing blue imbued with heaven's light.
Each foot is gently winged and to me flies,
And each a little dove with feathers white.
You hold my heart with hands that gently bear,
And lift my burning heart with you aloft.
And all I see in you is bright and fair,
As blushed with graces, sweet and lovely soft.
  But these are only just the graces seen;
  Your heart it bears a beauty much more keen.

# SONNET 91

The beauty of my words it matters not.
No matter what I truly promise you,
Or all the reasons I've before you brought,
You still remain unmoved by all I do.
You have resolved yourself to answer *No*
And now you'll never bend your heart and mind
To all the sweet affection that I show,
And I should leave my hopes for love behind.
   Yet still I hope, though love you have denied,
   For still I see the tremb'ling of you lip.
   I feel a falter that you cannot hide,
   As scales of love and doubt begin to tip.
   I see you want to give the answer *Yes,*
   Nor will you be content with any less.

# SONNET 92

How sweet is heard the fragrant sound of *Yes*
That stumbles quiet from your blushing lips,
As on my lips they warmly, softly press,
And from your mind all chilling doubt it slips.
How steady, strong, and firm the sound of *Yes*
And brings on whitened wing a fresh belief.
And all these words of love do in me stress,
But by my *Yes* I find my love's relief.
   And though you now withhold you tender *Yes,*
   And answer not the love that I express,
   And though your silence gives me keen distress,
   I still with patience do my love confess.
   I beg you, Love, do not your love suppress,
   But bless my aching heart with gentle *Yes.*

# SONNET 93

I know your mind and heart are wearied full
From hearing all my words of love and strife.
I know too many words will make a subject dull
As too much use will blunt the sharpest knife.
My songs of love are long and still grows strong.
And all my songs are all a praise of you,
But you would ask me halt and cease my song,
And this is what I've lately tried to do.
   But only lovers sing with heartfelt voice,
   And lift their joyous cries to God above.
   To sing or not to sing is not my choice.
   So I, by you, am bound to sing of love.
   And so my lover's song must still go on
   Until my hope in love is all but gone.

# SONNET 94

Though some may call me great in later days,
And greet these songs to you with great applause,
I count not much their high esteem and praise,
And give such fame no second glance or pause.
I have no care for greater wealth and fame,
And care not who may call me great or wise,
Or if they hold me up and sing my name.
It matters not if they tell truth or lies.
   I write these songs for you, my love, alone,
   To tell you all my love is my intent,
   And tell you how my love for you has grown,
   For every thought I have is on you bent.
   And measure of my greatness lies in you,
   And if again I gain your love so true.

# Sonnet 95

They say my every word's imbued with light,
They say my loving words are fair and true
And of the truths of love I give them sight
By saying all I see in eyes of blue.
They say I trace the brilliant burning heart
With just the words to say what I have seen,
And paint your face and heart with careful art,
With love and such devotion due a queen.
   But all my words fall short and miss their mark,
   And do not show you blushing beauty well.
   The words I use seem only bare and stark,
   And cannot all your love and beauty tell.
   Against your love and all your beauty fair
   No words I sing come close or can compare.

# Sonnet 96

These songs to me seem all a painful toil;
A daily trudge through swamp or piling snow.
A greater sadness 'round my heart does coil,
With every word my spirits sink more low.
I labor day and night with pen and page.
I toil through these words, but all in vain.
These songs are only just a pretty cage,
For I am trapped with only words and pain.
   I'd rather sit with you, and talk with you
   On love and light and things both old and fresh,
   As in the days before we used to do.
   I'd rather sing you all these things in flesh.
   But still I must content myself with thought,
   And think on all the lover's pains I've bought.

# Sonnet 97

Between the nights and days the distance grows
And makes our love more hopeless day by day;
For time is ever hungry, never slows,
Destroying loves that long forgotten lay.
With time your heart forgets, and mem'ry slips,
And lets me drift with half-forgotten dreams.
And soon you'll wipe my name from off your lips,
And soon forget the love that in me gleams.
 I beg you, Love, do not forget me yet,
 But wait for me as I still wait for you;
 For love that's left so soon will bring regret,
 And haunt your gentle heart your whole life through.
 I ask you for the sake of all we had
 And with a kinder light my mem'ry clad.

# Sonnet 98

Oh Love, your heart is crying 'neath the sky
And sheds an amber lighted evening tear.
It trembles with a bitter crimson cry,
A cry that cross the saffron sky does sear.
Oh Love, your morning light is dwindled now;
It once was breaking fresh and crisp with dew,
But now it dips out west with lowered brow,
And wanes to shadows deep and nightly blue.
 Take heart my love, and dry your evening eyes,
 Take up your waning light and with me walk.
 O Love of mine, take up your heart and rise,
 And leave these tears that in the darkness stalk.
 It's true I caused this evening now in you,
 But we could bring again a morning new.

# Sonnet 99

Oh Love, your heart is ghostly wan and pale,
A drifting phantom; ashen airy light.
It cries a wisping, shaking, haunting wail,
And hides in veils of vapor, vague and white.
Oh Love, you've lost your warmth and rosy blush;
And now the fire's drained from veins so cold,
And burnt to whitened ashes, pale and hush,
And all your love is by your logic sold.
  Oh Love, rekindle fired love in you,
  And find again the colors in you veined,
  And hued in you as rosy azure blue
  That's more than all the whisp'ring ghosts you've gained.
  Relight your color in my passions flame,
  With love regain the colors of your name.

# Sonnet 100

I here renew the purpose of my songs
And breathe again upon the cooling coal.
For still for you my heart so ardent longs,
And breaks that we're still broken, still not whole.
Your ears and heart and mind are wearied now;
I ask you still the course to hold and stay,
And heed the light my God my words endow;
I ask you listen still to what I say
  I here again confess I've wronged you love.
  I ask again for love and mercy sweet,
  And though I left you as a pinioned dove
  I wash again with tears you tender feet.
  Have patience, Love, and still your restless mind,
  And wait before you leave this love behind.

# Sonnet 101

My life's been blessed a thousand times and more,
A thousand graces given me from God.
I know His light still guides me as before
On all the darkened winding roads I've trod.
The life that's mine is filled with wholesome light,
And when compared with other lives is fair.
And I've been graced with brighter and mind and sight
And for me I have loving friends that care.
   And yet with life my heart is discontent,
   And finds it hard to see the light of day.
   With grief and pain my heart is bleeding rent,
   And restful in my chest it will not stay.
   Without you here my life seems long and bleak,
   And all the lights seem pale and vainly weak.

# Sonnet 102

My eyes are never closed in nightly rest;
My mind is never stilled within its course;
My heart is never restful in my chest
But stamps and rears just like a restless horse.
And by this constant vigil I am spent,
And tired close to giving in to sleep,
And all my aching heart is bowed and bent;
My soul is ever pulled to restful deep.
   I keep my vigil candle brightly lit
   With hope that you'll again to me return
   And by the window do I ever sit
   To trim my wick and wait for you and yearn
   As waiting for the coming bridegroom's train
   I keep my vigil though my strength may wane.

# SONNET 103

It seems as if my hope for you is gone,
And now has left me lightless in the dark.
And from my lamp the last of oil's drawn;
My coal has lost its heat and now its spark.
Despairs for you about me slip and drift
Opaque and dim as heavy shadowed haze.
And in this dusk the deeper shadows shift,
As faceless shades that fear in me does raise.
  Yet hope still springs eternal in my heart,
  As breaking dawn that spreads again its blush,
  And though the night may tear my hope apart
  The morning brings an amber lighted hush.
  By night my candle burns too low and fades,
  But morning bathes my heart with softer shades.

# SONNET 104

My changing mind sometimes amazes me
In charging to and fro so deft and swift.
With just a change of place and time I see
My mind will leap, and soon begin to drift.
I cannot keep my mind from turning back
To think on you, and things from brighter days.
I cannot flee when sorrow mounts attack,
As waves that toss my boat so many ways.
  I pray my Lord do ease my wearied mind
  And sooth the sore affliction of my soul.
  I only ask that I some peace may find,
  And make my mind again as one and whole.
  Oh Lord I pray you calm my heaving heart
  Before with change it tears itself apart.

# Sonnet 105

My footsteps linger long on weary feet,
And take me 'gainst my will from you away.
When first I ran to you my steps were fleet,
My steps are heavy now on leaving day.
And once my gaze was firmly fixed and true,
But now I cannot bear to look ahead.
And now a backwards glance I cast on you,
And will not follow signposts I have read.
   But fault me not because I walk so slow,
   For I still hope that you will call my name,
   And call me back, and ask me not to go,
   And maybe then forgive my mounting blame
   And so I wait with every step I take,
   And hope and pray that mercy in you wake.


# Sonnet 106

Indeed, I've forced my footsteps on their way;
I've tried to guard my eyes from glancing back;
I've struggled forward, trudging day by day;
I strain and pull myself along this track.
Your brightest love's transfixed my beating heart;
I've tried to now remove this stabbing lance.
I've tried by every means and strength and art
To break this spell of love and chaining trance.
   And yet I cannot exorcise your spell,
   The strength it holds me by is still too much.
   My firm resolve is only just a shell
   That cracks and breaks with just the slightest touch.
   And so I'll leave my leaving you behind,
   And pray my God enact his will and mind.

# SONNET 107

My heart is freed by you and I could go,
Unbound by obligations to your heart.
Now I can go wher e'er the wind may blow,
Or love again and make a better start.
This world is full of others I could find
And love again with just as deep a love.
And there are others just as bright and kind,
And there are more who shine as from above.
  But all these other loves to me seem dull,
  And shine as with a weaker light than you.
  My freedom too is not with light so full,
  And seems so faint and weak, and so untrue.
  And so I'll keep these chains that hold me fast,
  And sing their praises sweet until the last.


# SONNET 108

Now you my love are free as well from me,
And do not have to stay or love me still.
And from these chains of love you now may flee
And you may go from here when e'er you will.
I'm sure that you could find another love
To give you more than my devotion can;
And flies with whiter wings than does my dove;
You could be happy with another man.
  But could he love you as I truly do,
  Or hold you as I held you in my arms;
  Or bear his bleeding heart and soul to you;
  Or please your heart and mind with all my charms.
  For though he love you true, both fair and fine
  He'll never love you with a love like mine.

# SONNET 109

In times now past you loved me full and whole,
And loved with purer love than words can say,
And asked of me for love no tax or toll,
But trusted me and loved me more each day.
For you have loved as I have never seen,
With fragrant trust and great devotion pure,
As morning breezes blow both fresh and clean
With warming songs as morning's dove demure.
   I pray you not to let this beauty waste,
   Nor cast away your love or let it die.
   Do not with hold your love for fear or haste;
   Do not allow such love to pass you by.
   I pray you love again as once before,
   And I will love again but now much more.

# SONNET 110

Now think on all the stories that you've heard
Of lovers' hearts that strong and purely beat.
Who pledged their vows and stood then by their word,
And loved each other whole with love complete.
They would not stay their love for time or pain,
For grave injustice war, and distance great.
They died for love and bled their every vein,
And loved despite the pain of saddened fate.
   These tales are not for pleasure's sake alone,
   But teach us all to love more pure and deep;
   To move and break our hardened hearts of stone;
   And herd us back to love like wand'ring sheep.
   So heed these myths of love though they be old;
   Perhaps on hearing them you'll not withhold.

# SONNET 111

I've said before, more times than I can count
I've wronged greatly, this I say again.
Do not my deep remorse and pain discount;
I love you still as always, now and then.
This loss of love and faith is mine to claim;
I've snuffed the candle lit from passion's coal,
And for this darkened love I take the blame.
And all this weighs like millstones on my soul.
   Yet if you turned your heart and would relent;
   Awake the love that you have laid to rest;
   Then think of all the lighted graces sent
   To you in honor of your mercy blessed.
   So think of all the grace that you could gain
   If you but let our battered love remain.


# SONNET 112

I curse this distance that between us lays,
And harshly cuts me off from love and you.
I curse this time apart that grows with days,
That haunts each deep'ning night and morning new.
For here I cannot look upon you fair;
I can't caress you gently blushing cheek,
Or pass my fingers through your drifting hair;
Without the sight of you my heart grows weak.
   And so I send my love with wingéd dove
   I kiss your lips in song, though from afar
   And so caress your cheek with words of love,
   A love that time and distance never bar.
   So from afar I love you as I can,
   And love with just the humble love of man.

# SONNET 113

The deepest loves are never easy won,
And grow not full without much grace and pain.
And never are the lovers' trials done.
And easy loves become both cold and vain.
Our love has seen its share of trials hard;
Has fought through foes external or within;
And come through all these foes with love unmarred,
And by these hardships greater love will win.
　　So let us pass this newest hardship too
　　With confidence that love will still endure,
　　And last the night to find a morning new,
　　And in the moring find our love more pure.
　　If you would have a love more pure and fair
　　Then many loving hardships we must bear.


# SONNET 114

The pains that come with love are never few,
And plague the lover's life without reprieve.
Each day's a toiling trudge through trials new,
But with each restful night they closer cleave.
The lengthened years of love might seem a task
That taxes much the weary heart and mind,
And all these duties seem too much to ask;
An endless sacrifice by love assigned.
　　But every pain and effort that I take
　　Is made as sweet as honey to the taste.
　　And every selfless sacrifice we make
　　With gentle light like crimson gold is laced
　　By you and love my pain is made more sweet,
　　And with each sacrifice I'll gladly meet.

# SONNET 115

The birds when faced with winter's wind and snow
They spread their well fletchéd wings and swiftly rise.
On high flung winds they turn and southward go,
And with a windy haste they flee the skies.
Their haste is born of fear of coming cold;
They've heard the rumors from their northern kin.
In panic then their hearts are southward sold
And will not face the suff'ring that they're in.
I pray you not fly south with frightened birds,
Distressed by cold and hardship's frozen hand.
But take your comfort in my promised words,
And fearless face the icy wind and stand.
Though it be painful now to stand by love
I pray you love me still, my steady dove.

# SONNET 116

My soul is tossed and battered back and forth,
The winter winds have caught me in their course,
And I am driven, wrecked by screaming North,
And I am lashed by fate and nature's force.
Now all the birds that nested in my boughs
Have flown in fear before my wint'ry state.
They flew when first they saw my windy brows;
The slightest cold they'll not endure or wait.
But you, my halcyon1 dove, with me remain,
And make your nest despite the wind and cold.
You bring a calm to all my wint'ry pain,
With flashing feathers burning flaming gold.
I pray: endure these icy days of mine,
And wait for spring with warmth and graces fine.

# SONNET 117

The wrongs I've done to you have cut the rope
That bound our heart as one together whole,
And with the smudge of doubt have stained your hope,
And struck a blow to both your heart and soul.
And all the wrongs I've done might seem as proof
That show a lack of love and care for you.
For by my wrongs I've acted so aloof
It seems you're not the heart of all I do.
   But wrongs they only prove that I am man,
   And love you still despite my shameful crimes.
   As sinner loves his God as best he can,
   Though he may fall again for countless times.
   So do I love despite my fallen state,
   And on you mercy do I only wait.

# SONNET 118

My call is as a lover wand'ring lost
Whose rending heart is crying honeyed tears.
Like stormy skies at night by lightning crossed;
At once both dim and flashing bright appears.
My call is as a lover lost in love,
Transfixed by fervor's many passioned blades
And bound and chained to you, my whitest dove,
And lost to pain and other worthless aids.
With kindled words I cry my love to you,
With saffron words that scorch and burn my heart.
Ablaze and burning, cool as morning dew
I call as one who's almost torn apart.
   So heed my call, my love, and turn to me
   And do not veil your face and from me flee.

# SONNET 119

I know these songs I sing are sung in haste,
And all my words seem careless, tossed about,
As if I care not how my words may taste;
Or as a broken fountain, spit and spout.
My words are tumbled out and all confused.
I stop and start unsure of how they'll sound,
And by their length their weight is all diffused;
And in my songs no order can be found.
   But such a cry is as the lover sings
   As blinded by beloved grace and light.
   And when the sweet surrendered warmth she brings
   He makes a wordless cry upon her sight.
   And so I sing to you my loving songs
   To tell you how for you my heart it longs.

# SONNET 120

My heart is lanced, transfixed by passion's blade.
My heart it bleeds and all my mind is pain;
A torment every sight of you is made
By knowing I must still unloved remain.
The azure hue that kindly graces you,
And fills your eyes between your morning cheeks
Is as a two edged blade that cuts me through
And to my weak and bleeding heart it seeks.
   And yet I cannot flee or look away;
   Despite this lover's pain I'm fixed and still.
   No calm and reasoned words will make me sway;
   To run from you I have no strength of will.
   Relieve this desperate pain for you I feel;
   By some kind word or glance my burning heal.

# SONNET 121

Arise my love, my dove my faithful one,
And fly to me on rosy flashing wings;
For now the ice and winter's strength is done,
And all is filled with light and joyful sings.
Arise my love, my fairest dove and come;
Shake off these evening shades of growing night,
Do not to dark distrust and fear succumb,
But fly to me with willing wings of light.
   Arise my love, my fair and injured dove
    And let me bind, and heal your wounded wing,
    And heal the aching hurt I've caused your love,
    That once again our joyful hearts may sing.
    Do not now flee my kind and healing touch,
    For now your winging words protest too much.

# SONNET 122

I see your bushing cheeks and gentle lips
All painted in the evening lights of day,
When westward leans the saffron sun and slips
Beyond the azure hills and there to lay.
Your arms are like the slivered silken moon
That hold me softly through the darkened night.
Among the heaven's stars you're cast and strewn,
I see you in their silent silver light.
And every beauty that around me gleams
Reminds me of you face so gently warm.
And though I see you only as in dreams
I see you softly, fair in lovely form.
   Yet these are but a pale and shadowed taste,
    And can't compare when with you I am faced.

# SONNET 123

I'm falcon winged and plumed in silver dim;
On windy phantom dreams of you I rise,
And tempest forged, my eyes are keen and grim,
And in my dive more swift than arrow flies.
I circle sharp upon my pathless way,
Prepared to plunge at just the sight of you.
And yet on dreams I buckle here and sway
And airy 'bout me glide and and chill me through.
　But not with brutal strength my talons strung,
　Such deadly force will only do me wrong.
　I plunge with winging words; you beauty sung;
　My strength now lies in only just my song.
　I pray my falcon words are true and straight,
　And dive more swift, and come not now too late.

# SONNET 124

I'm now become a ghost and phantom form,
My limbs are pale and wan, and lost their weight,
I've lost the light and love that made me warm;
For such is my dim unrequited fate.
I now no longer speak with men on earth,
Or care for pleasures, rich and gaudy fair,
I see in them no value bright, or worth.
I'm now become a ghost as light as air.
　I beg you let your living mercy show,
　And lend me once again your warmth and light
　That I may burn again with earthly glow,
　And see again the world as warm and bright.
　　For mercy gives us breath on which we live
　　And so I beg you all my wrongs forgive.

# SONNET 125

I see the sunset, low upon the hills
With all its fragrant hues of softest bathing light.
From crimson challis flashing nectar spills,
And at the end of day it seems more bright.
I see the snowy veil with silver gleam,
I see the hills a purple lighted gem,
I see the glist'ning water in its stream,
I see the ragged edge of heaven's hem.
   And yet to me these all seem dark and dim,
   And grow more pale with every passing day.
   The beauty of this world seems edged and grim
   And passes, quick to darkness cast away.
   Without you here my world is faint and dark,
   And all is barren, bleak and coldly stark.

# SONNET 126

My hope was young and bright with morning's fresh,
With not a care for dwind'ling light of day,
And had its strength in spirit bright and flesh;
I thought that then it'd never fade away.
But now my hope is faint and growing old;
Its beard is graying hairs with growing strain.
My hope has lost its youthful valor bold,
And cautious has it grown from years of pain.
   And yet like Christ my hope will rise anew;
   Regain its strength and clear farseeing sight;
   Regain its faith and time-worn trust in you,
   And see the world again as fair and bright.
   For hope's not lost that you will love me still,
   And such a hope my mind and heart does fill.

# Sonnet 127

My love, your love is as my solid earth
That does not quake beneath my shaking feet,
And in your arms I find my love's rebirth,
And on you I have built my life complete.
Your love is rich as fertile soil dark
That grows again each year so fresh in springs.
There lives down deep in you a living spark,
Unquenched though rain and ice the winter brings.
　And though you're frozen now and veiled in snow,
　And will not sprout your lovely growing leaf
　Your love is steady still and growing slow.
　I hope and pray this winter will be brief
　And once again you show your love to me,
　And in our love we'll always steady be.


# Sonnet 128

My love your beauty is as waters clear,
So pure and soothing, cool upon my lips;
Untouched by earthly smudge and lustful smear,
And from your love it always softly drips.
Your beauty's stream is ever full and cool
And flows from springs where graces make their start.
It gathers in my soul a crystal pool
Where I have built a vessel of my heart.
　But I am parched and dried and thirst for you;
　For just a drop of soothing beauty's taste,
　For all the freshness of you morning dew,
　For I am all a burning scorchéd waste.
　So let me drink again your water pure,
　And let our drying love now still endure.

# Sonnet 129

My love your beauty is as breath to me,
As fragrant breezes blow up from the south;
Of chilling doubts and hazy fears more free,
And tastes of nectar on my lips and mouth.
I feel your love about me drifting soft,
To me an airy, whispered, warm caress;
That lifts my broken wings again aloft,
And 'round me do you gently breathe and press.
   Dispel these darkened mists that 'round me shroud,
   And breathe on me your beauty, soft and fair.
   Disperse this foul fog and choking cloud,
   And let me breathe again your clearest air.
   I pray you grant me air that I may breathe,
   And with your fragrant winds around me wreathe.

# Sonnet 130

My love, your love is as a brilliant flame,
That burns within my every lighted vein,
And fills me all with warmth at just you name,
And in its brilliance will it never wane.
As soft and sweet as amber lighted gold,
And gently lights the tinder of my soul.
And yet it flashes from you, bright and bold,
As crimson leaps from smallest smold'ring coal.
   My heart is cold and dwindles down to dark
   Without your warmth and flaming fragrance sweet.
   My heart is cold and lost its lover's spark,
   And dwindles now in frozen dark defeat.
   So let me now rekindle flames of love
   That we may shine with all the stars above.

# SONNET 131

Without you here I write as one inspired
By holy muse on fleet and wingéd feet.
And in my chest these words my love has fired
And so with holy help I sing you sweet.
My words do tumble out and overflow
As rivers burnished bright beneath the sun.
Without you here my words are never slow;
They come on eager feet and swiftly run.
  But when at last I see you face to face
  My words that praised you beauty once are fled,
  And I have lost my lovely muses grace,
  And can't remember all the things I've said.
  No words have I to tell your beauty true,
  For then my wish is just to gaze on you.

# SONNET 132

My heart is meek, contrite, and humbled low,
And turns not quick to think on sinful pride.
I fly not swift to envy's em'rald glow
That slowly grows with creeping oozing glide.
I care not much to softly lay in bed,
And think not much of pillows feathered fine.
And thoughts of crimson lust don't fill my head;
That set you in my heart as in a shrine.
  Instead my fault is found in too much hope,
  In hope that seems as phantom waning shade.
  And in this darkness now I blindly grope
  For just the thought that love might not yet fade.
  And yet I cannot help but hope in you,
  And so I'll keep this vice my whole life through.

# Sonnet 133

I've pled my case and told you all I know
Of parting pain that cuts me quick and deep.
I've told you how I waste days my so slow,
And how I pass my nights deprived of sleep.
I've told you how the darkness 'round me clings
With sharpened talons like some bird of prey.
I've told you how my heart in pining sings,
I've told you how I hope you heart will sway.
   And yet I know you've felt this parting pain
   As deep as I and yet more keen and stark.
   I know you've seen a life that ends in vain,
   And watched the faint and slowly dying spark.
   And so for sake of you and me and love
   I pray you fly to me, my dimming dove.


# Sonnet 134

You say our love and passions light has fled;
The sun has set upon our love and life,
And all the dreams we had are past and dead;
There's no becoming stronger than this strife.
You'll hold my heart no more in high esteem,
And love no more the light I lit for you.
And now no longer will you of me dream,
And will not pine for me or love me new.
   And yet I hear the longing in your voice
   That calls to me with words unspoken bright.
   I know you yearn for me against your choice,
   And long for me as eyes do long for light.
   You slight yourself if now you love me not;
   So make anew the brilliant love we wrought.

# SONNET 135

In older days when Homer held his seat;
When greater poets then still walked and breathed
They prayed to muses nine on gentle feet,
With light of heavens, soft around them wreathed.
And when these muses came with whispered song
To shed their light into the hearts of men
Then poets rose and sang their lyrics strong,
And then knelt down to pray for words again.
   But now I need no muse with flashing eyes
   To light my mind with words of love for you.
   No fickle muse can make my words more wise;
   Her words are vain and always far too few.
      But you, my love, are all the muse I need,
      And so inspire every word and deed.

# SONNET 136

I am not rich with gold and silver bright,
And have no gleaming jewels to stack and hoard,
And all I have is counted slim and slight,
And for the harsher days I have not stored.
I have no crown of gold and diamonds fair
To here bestow on you as you deserve.
I have no great estate of which to share,
And hold no hidden wealth in my reserve.
   Instead I only have my songs to give,
   Though humble in their making they may be,
   And fall unnoticed through the worldly sieve,
   And be cast off as just a lover's plea.
      These songs I give as diamonds of my heart
      And hope some wealth to you they do impart.

# SONNET 137

I watch these weary days slip slowly by
With patient mind and ever restless heart.
I look for omens in the birds that fly,
And sing your praises by my ceaseless art.
I labor now to make my heart more clean
And so prepare for you in me a place;
Adorning all as would befit a queen,
And fitting all with gold and silver lace.
   And yet you still delay your coming in
   And wait upon the threshold of my love.
   Now by this long delay my hope's grown thin;
   I pray you not depart my fairest dove.
   The night is cold with wind outside my door;
   Come in to warmth as once you did before.

# SONNET 138

I sit each sleepless night and wait for dawn
When golden sun will set the world ablaze.
Again the veil of night will then be drawn
And all the world a joyful song will raise.
I here endure the winter's talons keen;
Like all the world I long for coming spring,
When once again the earth regrow its green,
And every heart will once again take wing.
   So too I look for you and your return,
   Like melting spring and breaking dawn anew.
   I've kept my fires lit and always yearn;
   And with my growing flames I burn for you.
   So break on me like rising morning sun,
   And come again when winter's winds are done.

# Sonnet 139

My heart is starved and grows more weak each day,
Without the bread of love I slowly fade,
And from this famine I will waste away;
And so I ask for bread and mercy's aid.
My heart it thirsts for waters, pure and clear
That spring from you and o'er me sweetly roll,
And calms these parching pains that burn and sear;
And so I ask a drink to sooth my soul.
My heart is stripped and naked 'neath the sky,
And shivers pale without your clothing light,
And all the world will callous pass it by;
And so I ask for love like garments white.
   And do not pass me by and go your way,
   For only love and mercy now I pray.


# Sonnet 140

My heart is now unsheltered from the rain;
Exposed where once your shelt'ring heart had been;
Defenseless 'gainst the winds and wint'ry pain;
I pray your heart to roof me once again.
My heart is ailing, closer now to death,
And weakened by this loss of healing love;
And every day I fear my heart's last breath;
So visit me with mercy from above.
My heart is jailed and sees no more the sun;
Behind these bars of steel my love must dwell;
Behind the bars of all the wrongs I've done;
So visit me with mercy in my cell.
   Have mercy on my heart, my love, and come,
   Don't let your heart grow cold and icy numb.

# SONNET 141

My heart has grown distrustful, stained in doubt,
These doubts that creep in me and 'round me wīnd,
They cloak me all in darkness 'round about;
Dispel this growing doubt with mercy kind.
With love you gave my heart was lovely wise,
And knew all things as truly warm and bright.
But now my heart is lost 'neath darkened skies;
So come, instruct my heart with mercy's light.
My heart has wounded love and and lanced your heart,
And deeply pierced your soft and bleeding side,
And all our love my heart has torn apart;
So help my heart with gentle mercy's chide.
   I pray you work your mercy here in me,
    And give forgiveness light that I may see.

# SONNET 142

My heart is sore afflicted, plagued and strained,
There's no escape from torments that I see,
And only see that now your love has waned;
So let your mercy come and comfort me.
My heart has caused you pain by my offense,
And placed my crimes in me where love belongs,
And for these crimes I have no strong defense;
But let your mercy now forgive my wrongs.
My heart has caused in you a storming strife,
And great offense against you have I made,
And battered down the love that lit your life;
But bear these wrongs with patient mercy's aid.
   I only ask for mercy's softest hand
    That once again my heart might shameless stand.

# Sonnet 143

You say our love is dead and growing cold,
And by my hand your loving heart is slain.
There's now no spark of life that love does hold,
And all that's left is only needless pain.
And if, indeed, our love is past and dead,
And now no hope for health can here be found,
Let us have mercy on its soul now fled,
And lay it here to rest beneath the ground.
But not with weeping, tears, and wailing cries
But rather let us bury love with prayer.
To God above let us direct our sighs,
And lay our love to rest with hope still fair.
A burning hope that love will rise again,
And hope that we will find each other then.


# Sonnet 144

Again I say I place you not too high,
Or give more praise than you by rights deserve.
My love of God does not before you die,
For Him the highest throne I still reserve.
And though I see in you a light divine,
That gleams about your heart with gentle light,
Still brighter does the flame of heaven shine,
That burns with fright'ning beauty, blinding bright.
But still I see in you reflected grace,
That's captured in the azure of your eyes.
His light takes on the color of your face,
And through your light to Him I'll swiftly rise.
Your beauty gives me sight of God above,
And shines on me his burning grace and love.

# SONNET 145

The Lady Love is dressed in warmest light;
And walks with softest step through minds of men.
Her skin is fair her lips are soft and bright;
Her voice will call us all to her again.
Her cheeks are blushed with early morning skies,
And though the years of pain show on her face
In her a strong, unbeaten brilliance lies,
And all she does is done with kindest grace.
  And yet I love not Love herself but you,
  For you, her handmaid, are by far more fair.
  I cannot will her good as lovers do,
  And for my gifts she has no want or care.
  Such love of Love brings only tears and grief,
  And from such passion comes no pure relief.

# SONNET 146

The flashing Helen with her fairest face
Has not the beauty that you hold your own.
In her there's only just a passing trace
Of all in you the Maker's hand has sewn.
Not even Venus with her ankles white
Can match your tender beauty stroke for stroke;
Such swords of universal words are trite,
And 'gainst you Sophist mind is vexed and broke.
  I rather love *your* blushing beauty rare,
  A dark and light that only you possess,
  Imbued with grace that makes your *you* more fair,
  And I my own distinctive love confess.
  I love you with a love so rare and new,
  And love you full for just the sake of you.

# SONNET 147

Your lovely cheeks they blush with sunset hue,
A light no other cheek has every worn.
This rosy bathing blush I see in you
Is yours alone and from no other born.
Your eyes are fragrant stars of azure light
That gaze with softest glances all your own.
No other eyes are bright as yours are bright,
No other voice can sing with just your tone.
   But such distinctiveness does exclude,
   Does not deny the light of Heaven's grace.
   For by the light of grace in you imbued
   More clearly shine the features of your face.
   I love you, Love, in body mind and soul,
   And love the grace in you that makes me whole.

# SONNET 148

My love, your heart is bright with mirrored grace.
Reflected light from God and Holy Dove
That in your heart does find its resting place,
And shines from there that I might see and love.
Your eyes so well reflect this light to me,
And teach me how to speak His holy Name.
The grace of God and heaven high I see
So brightly shown within an azure frame.
   I too was once a gleaming mirror true,
   Though by my wrongs I've covered o'er my glass;
   Obscured the light I'm meant to give to you,
   But by His grace this darkness too will pass.
   I could again reflect if you'd forgive,
   And in a brighter light we both would live.

# SONNET 149

Your eyes are blue and bright and honest clear,
As skies on days when all that's seen is blue.
And stain of earthly pain can come not near
The sky descended down enfleshed in you.
Your eyes are azure, fresh and softly deep,
As seas when all the winds and waves have died,
And in those depths your shining pearls keep,
And in the calm of love to me confide.
 Your eyes are blue like Virgin's mantle soft,
 For by the Virgin's light they're made more pure.
 Like Virgin's grace they help me look aloft
 With grace and love both bold and yet demure.
 Your eyes are shards of Virgin's grace and light
 That shine in you, reflecting pure and bright.

# SONNET 150

Have faith in me that I will love you still
When all our days apart have slowly past.
May God again your faith in me instill
That we may love again until the last.
Have hope that once again our love will rise,
And burn more brightly now than did before,
And gaze again upon each other's eyes.
For hope in me and love I still implore.
 But more than these I ask of you your love;
 For love that burns with heaven's brightest flame,
 And lifts us both as one and whole above;
 For love that heals the darkened sin and shame.
  Without these three all love would have no worth,
  And by these three our love will find rebirth.

# POST SCRIPT

A lover's labor's never done till death;
For always will his love more brightly burn,
And so must sing his love with every breath
Until unto the ground he must return.
I'll never find my words enough for you;
For something more to say I'll always find
To praise your kindest heart and eyes of blue.
To me this lot of love has been assigned.
  And though these songs of you I now do end
  My blushing love, I still do sing and praise.
  And still I ask that you your ear may lend,
  And hear me praising you through all my days.
    So still I sing of you your love to win;
    I do my songs in earnest now begin.